LOSING A PET

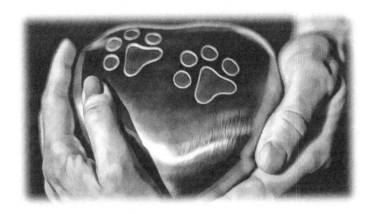

A Book of Grief & Recovery

The Pathway to Finding Joy After Pet Loss
When You Just Can't Get Over Losing Your Soul Pet

EMILY NEWCOMBE

Contents

Introduction 1

CHAPTER 1
Losing My Soul Pet: A State of Shock 7

CHAPTER 2
Learning from Life's Temporary Moments 21

CHAPTER 3
From Moments to Memories: The Transformation of Grief 31

CHAPTER 4
Honoring the Legacy 41

CHAPTER 5
Types of Pet Loss 51

CHAPTER 6
Disenfranchised Grief: People Just Don't Understand 75

CHAPTER 7
Rebuilding Phase: Embracing Life and New Beginnings 83

CHAPTER 8
From Darkness to Light: Pet Loss Can't Be Solved, but It Can Be
Survived 97

Conclusion 109

Get Your Free Bonuses Now!

As a way of saying thank you I'm offering a Guided Pet Meditation audio track and a Pet Grief Journal for FREE to my readers.

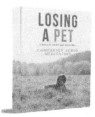 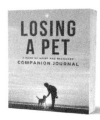

Bonus 1: Losing a Pet - Guided Meditation Audio Companion

- Exclusive audio content
- Meditative opportunity to understand and recover after losing a beloved pet
- 10 minutes of mindful reflection, relaxation, and stress relief

Bonus 2: Losing a Pet - Companion Journal

- Delve deeper into your emotional journey
- A private emotional outlet where you can process your grief in a healthy way
- 52 pages of healing prompts, encouraging and comforting quotes, and grief-related Q&As

Scan with your phone camera or go to: https://bit.ly/47Hj5NX

Introduction

"Cats, dogs, fish, birds, and others teach us more than we ever knew possible about love and, through their death, about loss. We come to know the best parts of ourselves through knowing them and are better for it, even if the price of such acquaintance is the inevitable pain we feel when they pass on."

— Kevin J. Coolidge

The loss of a pet is a universal experience that reaches into the very core of human emotion, yet it is one that society often underestimates or even trivializes. Whether it was a golden retriever that accompanied you on life's adventures or a quiet feline that graced your lap on peaceful evenings, their departure leaves a void that is palpable and, at times, overwhelming. A pet isn't just an animal that shares your living space; for many, pets are family, confidants, and irreplaceable companions in life's ups and downs. When they pass, the leash hangs idle, the food bowl sits empty, and their absence reverberates through daily routines, turning ordinary moments into poignant reminders.

This book is your guide through the challenging journey of grieving a lost pet. At its core, this is a manual of empathy, wisdom, and actionable advice. No two grief experiences are the same, but there are universal threads of emotion and coping mechanisms that can offer a blueprint for healing. Through a blend of science-backed approaches, heartfelt anecdotes, and practical tools, the intent is to help you find a pathway to joy—after you've allowed yourself to grieve fully and authentically.

It's not just sentimental words that affirm the intense emotional toll of losing a pet; research supports it too. A study titled "Grieving Pet Death: Normative, Gender, and Attachment Issues" detailed the psychological impact of pet loss and found that, for many individuals, the grief experienced can be as profound as the grief over losing a human family member (Wrobel & Dye, 2003). Such findings underscore the need for thoughtful support and coping strategies tailored to this unique form of bereavement.

The heartbreak of losing Belly and Sweepea was unbearable. In the aftermath of the loss, every corner of our home echoed their absence. The emptiness was more profound than I could have ever imagined. It wasn't just me feeling it—my family was grappling with the loss, and Rudy, our third dog, wore his grief as openly as any human could. Our shared spaces, once filled with the gentle patter of paws and joyful barks, seemed quiet and lonesome. It was during these trying times that I realized the need for guidance, understanding, and healing when it comes to pet loss.

Pet loss, as I've personally experienced, is not just about saying goodbye to an animal. It's about bidding adieu to a family member, a friend, a confidante, and a companion that stood by you through thick and thin. Belly and Sweepea were not merely dogs; they were the embodiment of joy, unconditional love, and boundless energy. They left an indelible mark on our lives. I remember the countless moments we shared—from the joyous occasions they were a part of to the quiet times when their simple presence was my personal solace.

However, life is a series of hellos and goodbyes, and while it's crucial to grieve, it's equally important to heal and find joy once again. So, how does one move past such profound grief? That's where this book comes in.

Every page of this guide is a testament to the immense love we, as pet owners, share with our furry friends. But more importantly, it's a beacon of hope for those seeking solace and healing. It's a promise that, while the pain might seem unbearable now, time, understanding, and perhaps a new paw to hold can bring back the lost joy.

Take my own journey, for instance. Just when I thought the void left by Belly and Sweepea was insurmountable, Lila entered our lives. This funky, playful pup brought our home back to life. It felt as if Belly and Sweepea had, in some mystical way, sent her to heal our broken hearts. Rudy, too, found a companion in her. Lila pulled him out of his depressive state and the transformation was nothing short of a miracle.

It's essential to understand that while our beloved pets may leave our side, they never truly leave our hearts. And sometimes, in the most unexpected ways, they guide us towards healing. Through my personal experience and the insights shared in this book, I hope to provide you with tools, understanding, and a new perspective on navigating the turbulent waters of grief.

Even in the darkest of times, there's a glimmer of hope, a pathway to finding joy once again. Through shared stories, tears, and eventually smiles, let's rediscover the joy that our beloved pets brought into our lives and find a way to celebrate their memory every day.

CHAPTER 1

Losing My Soul Pet: A State of Shock

"Until one has loved an animal, a part of one's soul remains unawakened."

—— Anatole France

The day started just like any other, filled with routine and the familiar sounds of our home. That morning, however, our lives took an unexpected turn. After a mundane veterinary checkup, our precious Belly, our first dog and soul pet, got diagnosed with stage 4 mast cell cancer. The words felt unreal, as if spoken in another language. They were hard to comprehend. Just days before, Belly had been her usual, vivacious self, playing with her toys, sunbathing, and looking at us with those big, expressive eyes. There were no symptoms, no warning signs.

Denial set in thick and fast. "She's been healthy. It must be a mistake," I kept telling myself. We hoped that, with the right chemotherapy medications, treatments, and a whole lot of love, Belly would pull through. After all, she'd been our anchor for the past 13 years.

But as the days progressed, small changes began to manifest. Once an embodiment of energy and zest, Belly began to pant more frequently. There were days when she seemed better, almost back to her old self, but then, just as swiftly, she would retreat, showing signs that not everything was right. My heart sank every time she displayed a hint of discomfort.

As days turned into weeks, our lively Belly transformed. The once voracious eater now stared blankly at her bowl. The energy to play, run, and embrace life seemed to have been drained out of her. The hardest part was seeing blood in her stool. Each time I saw it, I would retreat to a quiet corner of our home, tears streaming down uncontrollably. The thought of losing my best friend, my companion for over a decade, was unbearable. The cancer was finally taking its insidious toll.

Making the call for euthanasia felt impossible. How could I? But my spouse, seeing Belly's suffering and my own emotional turmoil, took that difficult step.

We wanted her last moments to be filled with love and as comfortable as possible. I remember the night before clearly. It was a gentle, calm evening. I fed Belly her last supper—scrambled eggs, the only thing she would try to eat at this point. Later, we took a quiet, contemplative walk, each step weighed down by the impending goodbye. I snapped pictures, took videos, desperately trying to capture every fleeting moment. That night, as we walked, the world seemed to stand still, with just Belly, the rustle of leaves, and me.

The morning of her final day arrived too quickly. With the vet scheduled to come over for an in-home euthanization, I took Belly for one last walk, cherishing every step, every sniff, every deep gaze of her eyes. Back at home, we settled her in her favorite spot at the foot of our bed, surrounded by her blanket and beloved toys.

Our children, too young to grasp the entirety of the situation but sensing its gravity, gently said their goodbyes. Tears streamed down my face, my heart heavy with sorrow, as the vet prepared for the procedure. A swift injection to the back of her neck and Belly drifted into a deep sleep. Just moments later, she was gone.

The void that was left behind was almost unbearable. Once filled with her joyful energy, the house seemed eerily silent. That state of shock is indescribable—a strange blend of disbelief, anxiety, and a profound sense of loss. Even the simplest tasks felt monumental. My throat would tighten and a dryness would take over, making even swallowing an ordeal.

The world felt distorted, as if I were viewing it through a foggy lens. Belly's absence was everywhere—in the silent corners, the untouched toys, and the empty dog bed. It was a reminder of the beautiful soul we had lost and the irreplaceable bond we had once shared.

A Deafening Silence

After Belly's passing, the silence in the house was unnerving. The soft patter of her paws against the wooden floor, the little whines she had made when she wanted attention, and her snorting as she dreamt during her afternoon nap were all missing. It was these little details about Belly that I missed the most.

Pet lovers will understand the importance of these little quirks. Each pet, no matter their color, size, or breed, has unique habits that endear them to us. Belly would always tilt her head a certain way when she was curious. Even as age brought a sprinkle of gray around her muzzle, her eyes would sparkle with youthful mischief. She also had the habit of taking two rounds around her bed before settling in, a routine she never broke.

You might be wondering why these details are so important to me. It's because these are the memories that remain vivid long after our pets are gone. Every pet lover cherishes these unique details about their pets because they aren't just animals—they are family members with their own set of quirks and habits.

The profound impact of Belly's absence was felt in the simplest of daily routines. Morning coffee had always been accompanied by Belly waiting for any crumb of my toast to fall on the floor. Her absence at that moment was louder than any words could be. Even something as mundane as the ring of the doorbell felt different because it no longer triggered her joyous barking while dashing to the front door.

The habits, colors, size, and even age of our pets all have a profound impression on us. A cat's peculiar habit of knocking things over, a bird's distinctive morning call, or a dog's uncontained excitement at the rustle of a food bag are the experiences that embed themselves in our memories.

As we continue in this chapter, we will delve deeper into these nuances. How does the absence of these familiar sights and sounds affect our daily lives? How can we cope when our day-to-day routine is suddenly devoid of these comforting habits? For pet lovers, it's these intricacies that keep us connected, reminiscing about our furry, feathered, or scaled companions. By understanding and cherishing these details, we can begin the journey of healing, one memory at a time.

Managing the Initial Shock of Loss

When a pet passes away, it's similar to a sudden solar eclipse on a bright, sunny day. A radiant, unwavering light unexpectedly fades, plunging our world into confusion and uncertainty. The impact of this loss is profound, and it shakes even the most resilient amongst us. To some, it feels like a sudden malfunction in life's machinery, compelling an unplanned halt and causing us to question our core beliefs about love and companionship.

Life with your pet was likely a tapestry of love, a constant source of joy and companionship. Their mere presence was a guarantee of affection, warmth, and unwavering loyalty. The familiar sound of their joyful bark greeting you, their endearing snuggles on lazy mornings, and their playful tussles with toys all contributed to a life enriched by their presence. But when that vibrant tapestry is suddenly unraveled, the emotional and mental void left behind can be overwhelming.

Losing a pet isn't just about an animal's passing. It's the loss of a trusted confidant, a cherished friend, and a beloved family member. Beyond their basic needs, we offer them a place in our hearts' most intimate spaces.

We confide in them, trusting their silent, unwavering loyalty and love. This heartfelt bond is what makes their absence so profoundly felt.

A Love Beyond Words

A child whispers secrets to an eager puppy; an adult seeks solace in the gentle purr of a cat; an elderly individual cherishes their final days with a devoted companion. These moments, experienced generation after generation, underscore the timeless bond humans worldwide share with their pets.

Considering our earlier discussions, it's evident that pets are more than just animals in our lives. They become our confidants, bearing witness to our highs and lows, all without passing judgment. They can be the beacon of joy on our gloomiest days, a testament to the indescribable emotional bond we share with them. Picture arriving home, wearied by the day's challenges, only to be greeted by gleeful barks or the soft padding of feline paws. Such moments dissolve the day's stresses, offering a sanctuary from life's storms.

For those unfamiliar with such bonds, the depth of emotions pets display might seem overstated. Yet, countless pet owners will vouch for their furry friends' uncanny ability to sense moods, offering comfort without uttering a single word. Their innate empathy and unwavering companionship make the grief from their loss even more noticeable.

Recognizing the depth of this bond is the first step toward healing. It's essential not just to mourn the loss, but to also celebrate the silent language of love that impacted our lives. Healing is a multifaceted journey, with each layer revealing its own challenges. By recalling the joy and camaraderie our pets provided, we allow ourselves to rediscover happiness.

Embracing Natural Order, Transitions, and Transformations

Life's beauty is marked by its impermanence. From sunrise to sunset, from the moon's cycles to the shifting seasons, the world around us continuously reminds us of life's transitory nature. All beings, our cherished pets included, embark on this finite journey.

Every moment with our pets—every playful nudge, every shared glance—becomes a part of our lives' fabric. Their presence is as familiar as winter's chill or summer's warmth. But change is inevitable, and understanding that is crucial.

The pain of pet loss can be immense. It signifies the beginning of a transformative journey—one of acceptance, understanding, and eventual healing. It's natural to grieve, to yearn for days gone by, but moving forward becomes an homage to the legacy they left behind.

Your memories of your pet are treasures that can illuminate even the most grief-stricken parts of your heart. Celebrating their life, cherishing shared moments, or holding memorials turns sorrow into appreciation. This transformation from grief to gratitude facilitates healing, and the shared memories become a legacy, a constant reminder of love once shared.

Every ending heralds a new beginning. Nature exemplifies this time and again—leaves fall to nourish the soil and sunsets pave the way for starry nights. Similarly, the void left by our pets can birth new memories, new bonds, and sometimes new pets.

Loss can be overwhelming, but recognizing it as life's natural ebb provides comfort. By acknowledging that all beings, ourselves included, are part of this grand cycle, we can find peace. Such an understanding allows us to honor our pets not merely as transient entities, but as everlasting presences whose imprints linger forever in our hearts. By accepting life's impermanence, we approach grief with a renewed perspective, making the journey of moving on more bearable.

Take, for instance, Natalie's bond with her cat, Mocha. Their evenings were filled with shared quiet moments—Natalie engrossed in her books, Mocha purring contentedly by her side. But when Mocha succumbed to pancreatitis, Natalie's house, once bursting with companionship, echoed with the deafening silence of loss.

Initially, many of us find it hard to accept the reality of loss. Our psyche tends to shield itself through denial, a temporary respite to process the shock. But this protective barrier doesn't last. As it fades, we're confronted with a wide range of emotions—from anger and guilt to profound sadness.

Basic daily routines become mountainous tasks. The familiar sounds and routines associated with our pets vanish, rendering our homes eerily silent, leading to a sense of dislocation.

It's crucial to recognize that these intense emotions, as overwhelming as they may seem, are natural facets of grieving. Acknowledging and experiencing these feelings is an essential step toward healing. And even as we wade through this emotional darkness, there's the promise of dawn—the light that eventually pierces through, illuminating our path forward.

Chapter Takeaway

Loving a pet deepens our souls and enriches our lives in countless ways. The bond, woven with shared moments and silent understanding, can be both joyous and heart-wrenching. The loss of such a treasured companion can shake us to our core, filling our world with silence and grief. But as with nature's cycles, there's a promise of healing and renewed hope. Embrace your emotions, cherish the memories, and know that, in time, your heart will find a way to heal and celebrate the love once shared.

Exercise: Mapping Your Emotions

Objective:

To understand and acknowledge the complex array of emotions you're experiencing during this difficult time.

Instructions:

1. **Reflect and breathe:** Position yourself in a tranquil space, free from disturbances. Make yourself comfortable and close your eyes. Inhale deeply through your nose and exhale slowly through your mouth three times. Allow yourself to be present in the moment.

2. **Identify your emotions:** Recall memories of your beloved pet. What emotions dominate your heart and mind? These emotions could include sadness, anger, guilt, loneliness, or possibly even relief, especially if your pet was enduring suffering. Recognize that these emotions, no matter how conflicting or confusing, are all valid. Grief isn't linear, and your myriad of emotions stands as a testament to its complexity.

Final thoughts:

Our emotions are a vast and complex sea that ebbs and flows, especially when grieving. This exercise serves as a compass, guiding you through that intricate maze, helping you recognize and validate your feelings. Emotions don't abide by any rules, and each individual's grief journey is unique. If this journey becomes too weighty or burdensome, remember that it's not a sign of weakness to seek solace or counsel, be it from loved ones or professional grief counselors. You're not alone on this journey.

CHAPTER 2

Learning from Life's Temporary Moments

"Some of us think holding on makes us strong, but sometimes it is letting go."

— Hermann Hesse

very living being moves to the rhythm of birth, growth, and eventual passing. This cycle, though natural, often seems abrupt and unjust, especially when we're faced with the loss of a cherished pet. Their condensed lifespans serve as poignant reminders of life's fleeting nature. As we navigate this chapter, we'll explore the universal truth of transience in greater depth. While we touched upon this difficult reality previously, we now aim to dive deeper, seeking understanding and solace in the natural order of existence. By embracing this perspective, we hope to find a pathway toward healing and rediscovering joy.

Recognizing Life's Fragile Dance

In the cycle of life, everything has a beginning and an end. From the tallest trees to the smallest insects, from mighty whales to fleeting butterflies, and indeed, even our beloved pets, every living creature has a finite existence. As humans, we often grapple with this reality, especially when it pertains to those we hold dear.

Imagine a garden. The beauty of a garden isn't just in its perennial plants, but also in the flowers that bloom for a season, bringing joy and color. They grow, flourish, and eventually wither, making way for new blossoms. This ever-revolving dance of life and death adds depth and dimension to the garden, making its beauty ephemeral, yet also lasting in our memories.

Similarly, the lives of our pets, though limited in years, are rich because of the memories and emotions they evoke. Their lifespans are considerably shorter than ours, and this reminds us of the delicate nature of existence. From gentle purrs to playful barks and wags of joy, everything remains as a cherished memory. The void left by their absence can be profound, but it also presents an opportunity to reflect and find comfort.

As you continue on your healing journey, consider engaging in activities that celebrate the life of your pet and the love you shared. Each memory serves as a gentle reminder of the bond that, although physically absent, endures in your heart. It is a tribute to the impact they had on your life, urging you to honor your memory by cherishing the times you spent together.

Many ancient cultures and philosophies, from the Stoics of Greece to the Buddhists of the East, have reflected upon the impermanence of life. They believed that understanding and accepting the transient nature of existence is a path to inner peace. By embracing this truth, they argued, one can lead a life filled with deeper appreciation, gratitude, and presence.

> *"Bear in mind that everything that exists is already fraying at the edges, and in transition, like actors beginning a performance and then bowing out."*
>
> — Marcus Aurelius, *Meditations*

In the modern age, with all its advancements and distractions, the timeless wisdom of these teachings remains relevant. When applied to the bond we share with our pets, it becomes a guiding light, illuminating the way we relate to them. It prompts us to celebrate the here and now, to cherish the simple joys, and to be fully present in the shared moments.

The pain felt when a pet passes away is, in many ways, a testament to the depth of the love that was shared. It's a natural response to the void left behind by their absence. But, by understanding the natural order of life, one can also begin to find solace. It becomes easier to celebrate the time spent together, rather than continuously lamenting the loss.

In the journey of healing, it's crucial to remember the beautiful moments, the lessons learned, and the unconditional love received. Rather than being a source of dread, the finite lifespan of our pets can be a reminder to love deeply, live fully, and embrace the present. In the end, it's not the years in a life that matter, but the life in those years.

Celebrating the Journey from Birth to Beyond

Life, in all its beauty and complexity, unfolds in phases. Just as the seasons transition, so too does the journey of every living being—through birth, the vibrancy of life, and the eventual return to the cosmos. The pain of loss may stem from a lack of acceptance of this universal cycle, particularly when it comes to our beloved pets. But acknowledging this rhythm can be a gateway to profound healing and understanding.

The concept of transience, especially concerning life and death, is as old as humanity itself. Ancient civilizations, philosophers, and religious scriptures have pondered it, seeking to understand and give meaning to our existence. What has emerged from these reflections is a shared understanding that life is fleeting, and that this impermanence is what makes every moment precious.

For many pet owners, understanding that their beloved companions have a finite time with them can be a challenging truth to confront. Yet, it's this very understanding that can also strengthen and deepen the bond. Whether it's the exuberant energy of a young puppy or the quiet comfort of an elderly dog, each interaction becomes a treasured memory, underlined by the knowledge that these moments are fleeting.

Pets, much like humans, undergo changes as they grow older. From the playful energy of their youth to the steadiness of their adult years and the slower pace of their senior days, they reflect the circle of life. These changes are natural and inevitable.

Of course, acknowledging this cycle doesn't make the eventual passing of a pet any easier. The heartache is still profound. But understanding that every living creature is part of this great cosmic dance can provide a sense of perspective. It's a reminder that death is but a transition from one form of existence to another.

Remember, grief is an indication of profound love. While the physical presence of our pets may fade, the essence of what they brought into our lives—the joy, the laughter, and the unconditional love—remains forever etched in our hearts.

Cherishing the Profound Imprint of Pets on Our Souls

In the stillness of quiet moments, when one sits by a window and the world seems to blur in the periphery, memories of the past surface, especially those connected to those we deeply cherish. Included in these memories are those of our pets who leave footprints on our hearts.

Even if their lifespans are but a brief chapter in our own longer stories, pets have an impact that goes far beyond mere companionship. They epitomize unconditional love, unwavering loyalty, and the art of living in the present. Through excited greetings, peaceful naps, and adventures together, they offer insights and lessons that decades of human relationships might not.

Consider the mornings when the world felt too heavy, and all that dragged you out of bed was the soft whine of your dog or the gentle nudge of your cat. These moments may seem trivial, but they reflect the anchoring role pets play in our lives. Their presence offers solace during times of distress, their innocence provides laughter on gloomy days, and their loyalty gives us a sense of belonging when the world seems completely foreign.

But just as they teach us about joy and companionship, they also introduce us to the harsh realities of life. Their shorter lifespans mean that we often witness their entire life journey, from their first curious explorations of the world to their final, serene moments. It's a harsh reminder of the inevitability of life's cycle.

As our pets age, their playful antics might become less frequent and their steps might become slower, but their eyes—those windows to their soulful spirits—remain the same. They shine with the same love, trust, and warmth, reminding us that while bodies might age, spirits remain youthful and vibrant.

As time moves forward and the sharp sting of loss becomes a dull ache, it's essential to remember the joy pets brought into our lives. Their memory stands as a testament to life's fleeting beauty and the indelible marks they leave on our souls. Their love and lessons remain intact, urging us to find joy again, even in their absence.

Chapter Takeaway

Life is a series of fleeting moments, each carrying its own unique significance. Our pets, with their shorter lifespans, underscore the transitory nature of existence. Their unspoken love, unwavering loyalty, and playful antics teach us to cherish the present. By understanding and embracing life's impermanence, we not only deepen our bond with them, but also learn to find joy and healing in every shared memory. Remember, it's not the length of time, but the depth of the moments that truly matter.

Interactive Exercises for Embracing Transience

1. Gratitude List

- **Description:** List the lessons and joys your pet brought into your life.
- **Instructions:** Write down 10 things you're thankful for regarding your pet. This could be anything from the joy they brought to lessons they taught you about life.
- **Purpose:** Gratitude can shift our focus from what we've lost to what we've gained.

2. Message to the Universe

- **Description:** A symbolic act of letting go and seeking peace.
- **Instructions:** On a biodegradable paper, write a message to your pet or a wish for your healing journey. If you feel comfortable, you can bury it in a garden or a pot as a symbol of returning to the cosmos.
- **Purpose:** Provides a tangible act of acknowledging your feelings, letting go, and seeking closure.

CHAPTER 3

From Moments to Memories: The Transformation of Grief

"Memories are the cushions of our past, turning sharp corners of grief into soft edges of remembrance."

— Eleanor Brownn

As we've explored, the transient nature of our pets is a poignant reminder of life's fleeting essence. When we lose them, we are forced to confront the lingering presence of grief and the shadow cast by their absence. But what if this very shadow could be our compass, guiding us back to the light? In this chapter, we will journey from the visceral immediacy of grief to the gentle embrace of cherished memories. With the passage of time, raw emotions mellow, reminding us that our bonds, though physically broken, endure in the heart's sanctuary. Through reflection and understanding, we'll seek to transform piercing heartache into a mosaic of beautiful moments, forever imprinted upon our souls.

From Heartbreak to Remembrance: The Healing Journey of Pet Loss

The bond between humans and their pets is a unique blend of mutual dependence, shared emotions, and silent understanding. We, as humans, often forget that our journey with our pets, while filled with moments of joy and laughter, also includes moments of sadness and inevitable separation. These creatures carve a special place in our hearts, and when it's time for them to depart, the void they leave behind can be monumental.

The loss of a pet is a heartache that's raw, unfiltered, and deeply personal. But, as with any form of pain and grief, it's also a part of the growth and learning process that life invariably brings. Over time, the raw edges of grief begin to soften, transforming into memories that provide comfort. They serve as gentle reminders of the times of joy, the days of play, and the moments of silent companionship.

This transformation from moments to memories is not an overnight process. It's a journey that requires time, patience, and, most importantly, self-love.

Imagine you're sitting in your favorite corner of your home. The lighting is just right—perhaps the soft rays of the setting sun are filtering in. You close your eyes and let your mind wander to the days when your pet was with you—the first time they looked into your eyes, the nights they curled up beside you, the mischief, the mayhem, and the moments of undiluted love. With each passing day, these vivid images slowly transition from heart-wrenching moments into comforting memories.

Saying Goodbye with Grace

Letting go is an act often laden with an overwhelming mix of emotions, particularly when it involves a pet. The furry friend who has been a part of countless adventures, rainy day cuddles, and shared silences now finds itself on the brink of a journey we cannot accompany them on. It's a testament to the strength of the bond and the depth of the love that saying goodbye is such an excruciating task.

The contemplation of their absence brings with it a tidal wave of sorrow, second-guessing, and a desperate yearning for just one more day. But as the guardians of these pets, there are times when the most loving thing to do is to allow them to move on peacefully.

Joan, a middle-aged woman from New York, once shared her painful journey of coming to terms with her beloved dog Max's deteriorating health. An energetic Golden Retriever, Max had spent 14 glorious years with Joan, bounding through Central Park, making friends, and bringing countless smiles to passersby. But as he got older, Max found it hard to keep up. As the vet visits increased and his pain grew evident, Joan grappled with the inevitable. "There were nights," she whispered, tears in her eyes, "when I'd hold Max close, willing him to understand that I wasn't ready. But he'd look back with those wise eyes, as if he were trying to tell me that it was okay, that he was ready."

The journey of letting go comes with bouts of denial, anger, bargaining, and profound sadness. Yet, interspersed are those moments of clarity, where our love for our pets transcends personal grief and decisions are made to keep their best interest at heart.

For some, the realization may come through spiritual or meditative reflections. For others, it might be through conversations with fellow pet lovers, or an introspective evening spent going through old photographs. In all these instances, there's an underlying thread of boundless love and a commitment to ensuring that our pets' final days are as painless and peaceful as possible.

It's said that when we adopt pets, we are signing up for heartbreak. Yet, every pet owner knows that the shared moments and the unconditional love far outweigh the inevitable pain of loss. Letting go isn't about forgetting— it's about cherishing the moments shared, celebrating a life lived with gusto, and understanding that, sometimes, love means saying goodbye, no matter how painful it might be.

Losing a pet is never easy, but letting go can be a transformative experience. As the pain subsides and the raw emotions settle, many find solace in memories, in the knowledge that they did right by their pets, and in the hope that somewhere, across the proverbial Rainbow Bridge, their pet romps in joy, forever free and remembered.

Remember, healing is a journey. It's okay to mourn, to feel, and to seek support, but in the midst of the storm, let love guide the way. It will ultimately lead you to a place of peace and fond remembrance.

From Loss to Growth: The Hidden Lessons in Grief

In the quiet aftermath of a pet's passing, amidst the sorrow and tear-streaked memories, there lies a subtle potential for growth and transformation. The pain and grief that accompany the loss of a beloved pet can seem insurmountable, but there's a unique strength hidden within this adversity—a metamorphosis waiting to unfold.

Pet owners often talk about the many lessons their furry companions taught them—lessons like patience, loyalty, and unconditional love. But what often goes unsaid are the lessons we learn when faced with their absence. The journey through grief, as difficult as it can be, has the power to reshape our perspective on life, love, and loss.

Consider the story of Liam, a gentleman in his 60s, who once shared his experience of losing his old tabby cat, Nala. Liam had shared over 18 years with Nala, and her sudden departure left a gaping void in his life. For weeks, he moved around like a shadow, the weight of her absence bearing down heavily upon him. But as days turned into weeks and weeks into months, something remarkable happened. Liam began to volunteer at the local animal shelter. It started as a way to fill the void, but soon it transformed into a newfound purpose. In his own words, "Nala taught me love in her lifetime, and she taught me purpose in her passing."

Such transformations aren't uncommon. While the journey through grief is deeply personal and each individual's experience is unique, the potential for growth remains constant. For some, it manifests as a renewed appreciation for the present—an understanding of life's fragility and the value of each fleeting moment. For others, it might lead to a deeper exploration of self—an introspection into one's beliefs, values, and priorities.

The beauty of such growth is that it isn't forced. It doesn't come from a place of "should," but rather from a place of "can." It's a silent testament to the heart's resilience, its capacity to heal, and its innate ability to find light in the darkest of hours.

While the idea of personal growth following a loss might seem counterintuitive, it's in these moments of profound sadness that we often find clarity. The barriers we erect around ourselves all crumble, leaving us raw, real, and incredibly receptive to life's myriad lessons.

For those navigating the treacherous waters of grief, it's essential to remember that it's okay to lean into the pain—to mourn deeply and fully. But it's equally vital to remain open to the lessons this experience might offer. As the old adage goes, "When one door closes, another one opens." In the context of pet loss, the door that shuts is undoubtedly painful, but the one that opens can lead to paths of understanding, compassion, and personal evolution that one might never have tread otherwise.

As time marches on, the sharp pangs of loss will gradually soften, replaced by a tapestry of memories woven with threads of love, laughter, and shared moments. And embedded within this tapestry is the profound potential for growth—a gift from a beloved pet and a testament to their lasting impact, long after they've left us behind.

Chapter Takeaway

Navigating the grief of pet loss can be an emotionally charged experience. However, within this sorrow lies the potential for healing and personal growth. Through time, the raw sting of loss softens, giving way to comforting memories that provide solace. The tales shared in this section reveal how moments of heartbreak can evolve into cherished remembrances. Letting go of a beloved pet, while painful, is a reminder of the deep bond and love shared. Embracing this pain, mourning deeply, and allowing oneself to be open to life's lessons can lead to profound understanding and personal evolution. As the journey progresses, the impact and timeless love shared with pets remain, guiding the way to peace and fond memories.

CHAPTER 4

Honoring the Legacy

"Love remains, long after the last paw print fades."

— Alex Sterling

Life has a profound way of connecting us with beings that touch the very core of our existence. These cherished companions—including our pets—leave a mark so deep that their absence creates an echoing silence.

Society's mixed perceptions about pet loss can sometimes cloud our understanding of our feelings. While the elation our pets bring is well understood and celebrated, the weight of their loss often finds itself on the periphery of societal empathy. The pain isn't debatable, however—it's real and deeply personal.

Honoring their legacy isn't about lingering in the pain, but rather embracing the love and memories they've left behind. In this chapter, we'll navigate the emotions surrounding pet loss and discover avenues to celebrate and remember our treasured companions. Through understanding, we find a path forward, ensuring their spirit continues to influence and inspire our journey ahead.

Cherished Companions

Pets have a profound influence on our lives, forming connections that are deep, transformative, and enduring. From the moment they step into our world, they shape our daily routines, influence our emotions, and teach us about unconditional love and loyalty. Recognizing their unique influence and role is essential, as it sets the foundation for understanding the depths of the connection we share with them.

1. **Emotional anchors:** Pets offer unwavering emotional support. Their mere presence can act as a balm on stressful days, providing comfort in times of distress or sadness. Their genuine affection and constant companionship uplift our spirits, reminding us that we're loved and valued.

2. **Teachers of life lessons:** Through their actions and behaviors, pets impart invaluable life lessons. They teach us about patience, resilience, and the importance of living in the present. Their straightforward approach to life, where joy is found in simple pleasures, is a reminder of what truly matters.

3. **Social catalysts:** Our pets often play a pivotal role in shaping our social interactions. Whether it's sparking a conversation with a fellow pet owner at the park or sharing stories and photos with friends, they often become central figures in our social narratives.

4. **A source of routine and purpose:** Caring for a pet brings structure to our day. Their feeding, grooming, and exercise schedules give us a sense of purpose and responsibility. This routine not only benefits their well-being, but also instills discipline and commitment in our lives.

5. **Physical and mental health boosters:** Numerous studies highlight the health benefits of having pets. They motivate us to be more active, lower stress levels, and even reduce the risk of certain ailments. Their playful antics can be a source of laughter and joy, instantly improving our mood.

6. **Deep bonds:** The relationships we share with our pets go beyond verbal communication. The silent moments, the understanding glances, and the intuitive connection highlight a bond that's hard to put into words, but that is deeply felt.

Acknowledging the multifaceted impact of pets in our lives helps us understand the depth of our bond with them. It's a bond that's nurtured through shared experiences, mutual care, and countless memories.

Celebrating the Legacy of Our Beloved Pets

Amidst the grief and sorrow of pet loss, it is essential to find ways to celebrate their lives and honor the profound impact they have had on our existence. Here are some meaningful ways to remember and pay tribute to our treasured companions:

1. **Memorial spaces:** Create a dedicated corner in your home with their favorite toys, photographs, and even their ashes. This space serves as a tangible reminder of the time you spent together and a place to reflect on the memories.

2. **Tribute art:** Commission a portrait or sculpture of your pet. Art captures the essence of your beloved companion in a timeless form, allowing you to cherish their image and spirit for years to come.

3. **Journaling:** Pen down your thoughts, memories, and feelings associated with your pet. Writing can be a therapeutic process, helping you process grief while preserving memories.

4. **Plant a tree:** Choose a sapling and plant it in your pet's honor. As the tree grows, it stands as a living symbol of the growth and nurturing nature of your bond.

5. **Volunteering and donations:** Spend time volunteering at animal shelters or make a donation in your pet's name. Such acts not only honor your pet's memory, but also support other animals in need.

6. **Memorial events:** Organize a gathering of friends and family to celebrate the life of your pet. Share stories, photos, and memories, reinforcing the idea that your pet's legacy is not only cherished by you, but also by those around you.

7. **Custom jewelry:** Create custom jewelry pieces, like a locket with your pet's photograph or a pendant with their paw imprint. Wearing them keeps your pet close to your heart, both figuratively and literally.

8. **Digital tributes:** Use social media platforms or create a dedicated website to share memories, photographs, and stories of your pet. Such platforms allow a broader audience to understand and appreciate the special bond you shared.

Grieving the loss of a beloved pet is a long journey. By celebrating their life and the memories you created together, you pave a path to healing and acceptance. Their legacy remains alive in the love they gave, the lessons they taught, and the moments you shared. Remembering and honoring them is an acknowledgement of the indelible mark they left on our hearts.

Processing Grief: Finding Light After Loss

Grief, in all its forms, can be a heavy burden to bear. When we lose a pet, we lose a presence in our lives that brought moments of joy, companionship, and routine. While the depth of connection varies for each individual, the experience of loss is universal.

The immediate aftermath of such a loss can be disorienting. The spaces our pet once occupied might seem emptier, and our routines may feel disrupted. But as with any form of grief, the pain gradually evolves, transforming into a blend of memory and acceptance.

It's human nature to hold onto moments of the past and replay them in our minds, especially when they're associated with happier times. Remembering a pet's playful antics or curious nature is a part of the healing process. However, it's also essential to ground ourselves in the present, recognizing that life continues.

Finding a balance between cherishing the past and embracing the present is key. This can be achieved by establishing new routines, exploring hobbies, or even just allowing oneself the time and space to process feelings. It's okay to miss the presence of a pet, but it's also okay to find joy in new experiences.

Sometimes, channeling our emotions into tangible actions can be therapeutic. This could be as simple as creating a photo album, planting a tree in their memory, or donating to a local animal shelter. These acts are not about replacing the past, but celebrating the continuity of life.

There might be days where the weight feels a bit lighter, and others where it returns with a renewed intensity. During these moments, it's crucial to be patient with oneself and to understand that healing is a process, not a destination.

Loss is an inevitable part of the human experience. It shapes us, teaches us about the fragility of life, and underscores the importance of appreciating the present. With time, the memories of our pets will blend with the fabric of our lives, reminding us of the moments of joy they brought and the resilience of the human spirit, which can find light, even after the darkest days.

Chapter Takeaway

Pets shape our daily experiences and emotions in countless ways. The depth of the impact of loss is profound, affecting our emotions, life lessons, social interactions, routines, health, and intangible bonds. When we face the inevitable pain of their loss, it's not about lingering in grief, but cherishing and celebrating the rich legacy they've left behind.

From creating dedicated memorial spaces to writing down our feelings, there are numerous ways to honor and remember our treasured companions. Navigating the journey of grief requires a balance of embracing past memories and living in the present. By channeling emotions constructively and allowing ourselves the time to heal, we can gradually find solace. We honor our pets by cherishing the moments of joy they have brought into our lives and recognizing the resilience of the human spirit.

CHAPTER 5

Types of Pet Loss

"Every type of pet loss is a chapter in the book of love we shared with them."

—— Jordan Hayes

ollowing our journey of personal grief, introspection, and honoring our pets, we arrive at a deeper exploration of the varied faces of pet loss. While my own narrative revolves around the shocking departure of my soul pet, I've come to recognize that each person's tale of loss bears its own nuances, each uniquely heart-breaking.

During our previous discussions, we've seen how life's transitory moments shape our bonds with our pets, and how these moments transition into lasting memories that influence the very essence of our grieving process. We've also recognized the importance of commemorating these beautiful creatures who've touched our lives so deeply.

In this chapter, we'll explore the different types of pet loss, giving voice to the various feelings you might be grappling with. Whether it's the suddenness of an unexpected accident or the prolonged pain of witnessing a pet's health decline, each type of loss has its own set of emotions and challenges. By understanding these distinctions, we seek to provide solace—to assure you that your grief, in all its forms, has a place in the vast tapestry of shared human experience.

As we navigate this journey, bear in mind that the categories we discuss are merely waypoints, guiding us toward empathy and mutual understanding. They don't limit or define your grief, but offer a hand to hold as you walk through your healing journey.

Navigating the Painful Choices and Embracing Farewells

The journey of pet ownership is a mosaic of joyful memories, shared adventures, and deep bonds. Yet, in this beautiful tapestry, there are threads of pain and heartbreak. I found myself traversing one such thread when my beloved pet's health began its decline. This chapter is a reflection on my intimate experience with anticipated pet loss, the emotional maelstrom it evoked, and the path I took towards understanding and healing.

A Slow Dawning of Realization

Time is a relentless force, and as time passed, subtle changes began to manifest in my beloved Belly. The vigor of youth gradually gave way to the mellowness of age. It's a transition many pets undergo, but the real storm clouds began to gather when the word "illness" entered our vernacular. The diagnosis of "stage 4 mast cell cancer" was more than just a medical term; it was a cruel reminder of the fragility of life.

The Importance of Quality of Life

In the wake of the diagnosis, our home became a fortress against the onslaught of the disease. Medications, therapies, and countless vet visits punctuated our days. Yet, throughout this ordeal, my focus remained fixed on one thing: Belly's quality of life. Her joy in the simple things, her appetite, and her moments of play became my daily metrics. Conversations with our veterinarian became essential touchpoints, guiding me in understanding and ensuring Belly's comfort.

Euthanasia: The Hardest Decision

Few words in the pet owner's lexicon carry as much weight and emotional charge as "euthanasia." I grappled with it, wrestled with its implications, and felt its immense gravity. It's a decision no pet owner wishes to face, yet it is an indication of the profound love we bear for our pets. It's a choice to end pain and offer peace, even if it shatters our hearts in the process.

The Emotional Quicksand of Guilt

Doubt and guilt were persistent companions in the aftermath. Questions plagued me. "Was it too soon?" "Could I have done more?" The reassurance of friends and the wisdom of professionals provided some solace, but it was a journey of internal reconciliation, of coming to terms with the fact that decisions made out of love can never be wrong.

Saying Goodbye: My Moment with Belly

Our home, once a playground for Belly's antics, transformed into a sanctuary of reflection and memories. Her companion, Sweepea, seemed to mirror my emotions, offering silent companionship as the weight of the impending farewell bore down on us. That final morning, time seemed to stand still. Our home was a cocoon of love, memories, and shared experiences. As I held Belly close, our bond transcended words. It was a silent pact, a promise to cherish, remember, and honor our shared journey.

Anticipated pet loss is a challenging road, lined with pain, introspection, and profound love. Through my experience with Belly, I learned that while the pain of parting is deep, the love we share and the memories we create are eternal.

Navigating the Unanticipated Farewell

The profound bond between a pet and its owner is built on countless shared moments of joy, laughter, and trust. But when an unexpected event leads to the sudden loss of a cherished pet, the immediate aftermath can be overwhelming. Sudden losses, in contrast to anticipated ones, offer little time for mental preparation or final goodbyes.

The Shock and Disbelief

When a pet is taken suddenly, the initial reaction is often shock and disbelief. The spaces where the pet once roamed appear larger, and the home seems engulfed in silence. There's a noticeable void, one made even more profound by the abruptness of the departure.

Understanding the Circumstances

Accidents and unforeseen health crises are among the most common causes of sudden pet loss. A pet might ingest a harmful substance, become a victim of an unfortunate accident, or face a sudden, aggressive ailment that gives little warning. The unexpected nature of such events adds a layer of complexity to the grieving process, as owners grapple with questions of "why" and "what if."

The Emotional Whirlwind

Beyond the shock lies a spectrum of emotions. Guilt, anger, regret, and a deep sense of loss often converge, making the grieving process intricate and, at times, confusing. The absence without prior warning means there's no opportunity for gradual acceptance, so emotions hit hard and fast.

Jen's Heartrending Experience

Amid this emotional turmoil, we come across stories like that of Jen. For her, a routine decision turned tragic when her trusted pet sitter allowed her dog off the leash in an unfenced park. Since that day, her dog hasn't been seen. The grief Jen faces is unique, as it's marked by the uncertainty of not knowing. Every unanswered call, every passing day without a sign, amplifies the sense of loss. Her quest isn't just to locate her pet, but also to navigate the emotional maze of hope, despair, and the ambiguity of her situation. Her journey serves as an example of the vulnerability and unpredictability of life.

Moving Forward: Strategies for Healing

Sudden losses require a distinctive approach to healing. Here are some suggested steps:

1. **Allow yourself to grieve:** Understand that the feelings of shock, anger, and sadness are natural. Give yourself permission to feel and process these emotions.

2. **Seek support:** Surround yourself with understanding friends or family. Consider joining support groups or seeking professional help to navigate your feelings.

3. **Memorialize your pet:** Celebrating your pet's life through memorials or remembrances can offer solace.

4. **Avoid self-blame:** While it's natural to wonder if you could have done things differently, it's essential to understand that accidents and unforeseen events are, by their very nature, unpredictable.

5. **Give it time:** Healing is a journey, not a destination. Time can soften the pain, even if the memories remain.

The Cumulative Grief of Multiple Losses

Loss in any capacity can be deeply traumatizing. The pain can ripple through our lives, causing profound emotional distress. When one has to endure the heartbreak of losing multiple pets in a short period of time, the feelings can be overwhelmingly intense and the cumulative grief can be complicated to navigate.

The challenges of experiencing multiple losses within a short time frame can be multifaceted:

1. **Intensity of emotions:** The emotions you feel after losing one beloved pet are compounded by the addition of another loss. Instead of having time to heal from one loss, you're immediately thrust into another wave of grief. This can lead to heightened feelings of sadness, guilt, and sometimes even anger.

2. **Cascading memories:** Every pet brings with it a plethora of memories. The loss of multiple pets means not only coping with the immediate grief, but also confronting an influx of memories from each pet, which can be emotionally draining.

3. **Perceived inability to cope:** With one loss, there is a path to healing, even if it's hard to see in the

immediate aftermath. With multiple losses, that path can seem obscured, leaving individuals feeling lost and unsure of their emotional resilience.

When grappling with the loss of multiple companions, the grieving process can sometimes feel like waves crashing over you, one after the other. It's essential to recognize this and give yourself the time and space needed to mourn each loss.

For those seeking strategies to cope with multiple pet losses:

1. **Separate the grief:** While it might seem like the grief is one massive entity, it can be therapeutic to separate the grief for each pet. By doing this, you allow yourself to mourn each pet individually and cherish the unique memories you had with each one.

2. **Seek support:** Surrounding yourself with understanding friends, family, or support groups can be invaluable. Sharing stories, memories, and feelings can offer solace and a sense of understanding.

3. **Create memorials:** Setting up a small memorial for each pet, such as a photo collage or a dedicated space in your home, can help preserve their memories and give you a place to reflect.

4. **Allow time:** Healing does not happen overnight, especially with compounded grief. Give yourself time, and don't rush the process. Everyone heals at their own pace.

Lorena's Tragic Incident with a Coyote

In a quiet suburban neighborhood, tragedy struck Lorena when a coyote managed to breach her backyard fence. Her two young puppies, merely 2 and 3 years old, were unsuspecting victims. Lorena had enjoyed watching them play in the yard, enjoying their little baths and frolics under the sun. The incident was swift and devastating.

Lorena was consumed with guilt and sadness. Thoughts like, "Why did I leave them outside?" and "How could I not protect them?" clouded her mind. The emptiness felt all-consuming, and every corner of her house seemed to echo with their absence. It was as if a veil of sorrow had draped itself over Lorena's world.

Such events are an unfortunate reminder of the unpredictability of life. The external environment can sometimes pose threats that we may not always foresee. The key was for Lorena to remember that such incidents are not a reflection of her love or care for her pets. They are a cruel twist of fate. While the pain may seem unbearable, it is crucial to seek ways to cope and eventually find a path to healing.

Confronting the loss of multiple pets is an emotional journey, one that requires compassion, patience, and understanding. Whether you're supporting someone like Lorena through her grief or navigating your own, remember that healing is possible, even if the journey seems long and arduous.

Children and Pet Loss: Guiding Young Hearts Through Grief

Pets play significant roles in a child's life, offering joy, comfort, and valuable lessons about care and responsibility. When a cherished pet is no longer around, the void that remains can feel immense, especially for young hearts unfamiliar with the concept of loss.

Understanding a Child's Grief

Depending on their age and maturity, children process grief differently than adults. For some, the death of a pet might be their first encounter with mortality. Their reactions can range from confusion and sadness to anger or even seeming indifference. Younger children might not fully comprehend the permanence of death and may expect the pet to return. They could have questions about where the pet has gone or if it might come back. Older children, on the other hand, might understand the finality, but struggle with overwhelming emotions or the unfairness of the situation.

Offering Age-Appropriate Support

1. **Toddlers and preschoolers:** At this age, children have a limited understanding of death. They might see it as a temporary situation, akin to sleeping. When explaining the loss, it's essential to use simple, clear language. Avoid euphemisms like "put to sleep," which can be confusing. Instead, say, "Our pet won't come back." Encourage them to express their feelings through drawings or play, which are natural mediums of expression for them.

2. **Elementary-aged children:** Kids in this age group begin to grasp the permanence of death, but might personify it as a monster or villain. They might also feel guilt, thinking they did something to cause the pet's death. Reassure them with consistent and honest explanations, allowing them to share their feelings and memories.

3. **Pre-teens and teens:** This group tends to understand death similarly to adults, but might

struggle with expressing their emotions. They might prefer to grieve privately or with peers. Offer them the space to mourn, while also letting them know that you're there for them.

Encouraging Open Communication

Open dialogue is vital. Encourage children to speak about their pets, share memories, and ask questions. This open conversation creates a supportive environment, letting them know that their feelings are valid and that it's okay to grieve.

Tools to Aid Understanding and Grieving

1. **Books about pet loss for children:** There are numerous books for children that address pet loss. These can provide a framework for understanding and processing their feelings.

2. **Memory boxes:** Create a memory box with your child, where they can keep mementos like collars, photos, or toys. This tangible reminder can be a source of comfort.

3. **Art and writing:** Encourage children to draw pictures or write stories about their pets. This creative outlet allows them to celebrate the bond they had and process their emotions.

In the wake of a pet's passing, it's crucial to acknowledge and respect the unique way each child processes their grief. With patience, understanding, and open communication, we can guide them through this challenging experience, ensuring they emerge with coping tools they can use throughout their lives.

Solitude and Pet Loss: Navigating Grief Without a Support Net

For many, pets offer a warmth that goes beyond that of human interaction. They're silent listeners, non-judgmental companions, and loyal friends. When an individual without a broader familial support system loses such a precious bond, the world can suddenly seem unbearably quiet.

The Echoing Silence of Loss

When a pet is one's primary source of companionship and emotional support, its loss can create a vacuum. That echoing silence can amplify feelings of loneliness and isolation, making the grieving process even more challenging. The routines—the feeding, the walking, and the playing—that were once full of life now feel like stark reminders of what's missing.

Reaching Out: The First Steps to Healing

For those without an immediate family or support structure, the process of grieving can feel insurmountable. However, human connection, even if it's not familial, can play a crucial role in the healing journey.

1. **Friends and acquaintances:** It might be a daunting task to share feelings with someone, but reaching out to even a distant friend can make a world of difference. You might not replace the pet, but you can offer a listening ear and a momentary distraction.

2. **Neighbors:** Neighbors often see our daily routines, especially with our pets. A simple conversation, sharing memories, or just the acknowledgment of the loss can make one feel less alone.

3. **Community groups and pet bereavement circles:** Many towns and cities have groups for those who've lost pets. These circles understand the pain and offer a space to grieve, share stories, and heal together.

4. **Online support networks:** In today's digital age, one can find numerous forums, groups, and platforms dedicated to pet loss. Sometimes, just reading others' experiences can offer solace.

Alex's Journey Through Silence

In a bustling city, Alex led a life that many would describe as "lonely." But for Alex, it was enough, for he had Bruno, a golden retriever with fur as radiant as the sun. Bruno was not just a pet, but also a lifeline—the heartbeat of Alex's home and the joy of his life.

When Bruno passed away suddenly, the loss was deafening. The apartment felt colder, the nights longer, and the silence unbearable. With no family to lean on and a reserved nature, Alex initially sank into the depths of grief, feeling adrift in a vast ocean of sorrow.

However, during one of his solitary walks (an old routine he and Bruno would often do), Alex stumbled upon a community group gathered in a park, sharing stories of their pets, both living and lost. He approached hesitantly and soon found himself enveloped in stories, laughter, tears, and shared memories. Over time, this group became Alex's refuge, helping him navigate his grief and rebuild his life, one step at a time.

For Alex and countless others, the message is clear: While the loss of a pet can plunge one into profound solitude, there is always a world out there full of understanding hearts and open arms. It takes courage to reach out, but when you do, the journey from grief to healing becomes a shared endeavor, proving that, even in loss, one is never truly alone.

Nurturing the Healing Hearts of Surviving Pets

Just as humans grapple with the complexities of grief, the animals left behind also experience the anguish of loss. Their understanding of the world is largely based on routines, scents, and companionship. And when one of their own is suddenly missing, they too can feel the void.

Reading the Silent Cues of Distress

Surviving pets may not express their grief in words, but their behavior often provides subtle indicators. Changes in their daily habits, a decline in appetite, a reluctance to play, or a persistent search for the departed companion are all possible manifestations of their grief. A cat that was once vocal might retreat into silence, while a playful dog might lose interest in his favorite toys. Observing these nuanced shifts is essential for a pet owner, as they are the first signposts pointing to a pet's inner turmoil.

Lending an Understanding Ear

Empathy plays a pivotal role at this juncture. It's vital to ensure that the surviving pets receive ample affection and comfort. Extra cuddles, gentle words of assurance, and maintaining their routine as much as possible can be profoundly reassuring for them. They need to feel stability, especially when the world seems a little emptier.

Reintroducing Social Bonds

Isolation, even for a grieving pet, can exacerbate feelings of loneliness. Encouraging interaction with other animals or taking them to pet-friendly parks or events can help. These environments often provide distractions, and the sheer act of observing or engaging with other animals can rekindle their spirit. Additionally, it might also be a good opportunity for owners to connect with fellow pet enthusiasts, leading to mutual emotional support.

Introducing a New Pet

The decision to introduce a new pet following a loss is deeply personal and should be navigated with sensitivity. While a new pet can bring joy and liveliness to a home, it is essential to ensure that the timing is right for both the surviving pet and the owner.

Before bringing in a new pet, one should evaluate the readiness of the surviving animal. Are they showing signs of being more receptive to companionship, or are they still in a state of distress? Sometimes, introducing a new pet prematurely can lead to territorial disputes or further stress.

When the time does feel right, the introduction should be gradual. This can involve supervised meetings in neutral territories before they share the same space. Over time, with patience and understanding, new bonds can form, filling the home with renewed energy and hope.

In the wake of loss, life can feel fragile and unpredictable. Yet, as pet owners and their surviving pets navigate the turbulent waters of grief together, a deeper bond often emerges. It's a testament to the resilience of love, reminding everyone involved that, even in the shadows of sorrow, the light of healing awaits.

Beyond Companionship: The Loss of a Service or Therapy Animal

Service animals, therapy pets, and emotional support animals play an indispensable role in the lives of many individuals. Their presence has a profound influence, often facilitating physical mobility, offering emotional stability, or even saving lives. The bond between a person and their service or therapy animal is unlike any other— it's not just about companionship, but also about trust, dependency, and a deep mutual understanding.

The Importance of Service and Therapy Animals

Service animals are trained to perform specific tasks that cater to the disabilities of their owners. This could include guiding the visually impaired, detecting impending seizures, or aiding those with mobility challenges. Therapy pets, on the other hand, are employed in therapeutic settings, providing comfort to individuals in hospitals, nursing homes, or counseling sessions. Emotional support animals serve to alleviate symptoms of emotional or psychological conditions.

For many, these animals are life-enhancing partners— navigating the world with them, providing an anchor in times of emotional upheaval, or even becoming the bridge that facilitates social connections.

Confronting the Void

When such an essential being departs, the aftermath can be devastating. Beyond the pain of losing a beloved companion, there's the absence of a being that provided physical aid, emotional stability, or a combination of both. Daily routines can be disrupted, and the owner might feel an intensified sense of vulnerability or isolation.

Sarah and Echo

Sarah, a young woman with a hearing impairment, had Echo, a service dog, by her side for seven years. Echo was trained to alert Sarah to specific sounds, like doorbells, alarms, or someone calling out to her. Their bond transcended the normal human-animal interaction. For Sarah, Echo was her ears, her guardian, and her confidant.

When Echo passed away unexpectedly, the silence in Sarah's life became more pronounced. The absence of her furry sentinel made her home feel vast and empty. Without Echo, every missed doorbell or unheard call became a painful reminder of her loss.

With time, and with the support of her close-knit community, Sarah began attending group therapy sessions for individuals who had lost service animals. Sharing her pain, listening to others, and being understood in an environment where everyone recognized the depth of such a loss began her journey to healing.

Chapter Takeaway

After the loss of a service or therapy animal, the journey forward is about finding new adaptations, understanding that grief has its own pace, and eventually realizing that, while the beloved animal can never be replaced, the heart has an immense capacity to heal and love again.

Throughout this chapter, we've explored the multifaceted experience of pet loss—from the sudden departures that jolt our being to the unique pain of losing service animals that played pivotal roles in our daily lives. In every instance, the recurrent theme is love, dependence, and the inevitable pain of loss. Yet, within these experiences also lie hope, resilience, and the undeniable strength of the human spirit. As we journey ahead, remember that every pain carves a space within us, and that this space can eventually be filled with understanding, growth, and renewed joy.

CHAPTER 6

Disenfranchised Grief: People Just Don't Understand

"Validating another's grief is a profound act of kindness; for in recognizing their pain, we acknowledge their love."

— Dr. Fiona McCullough

Grief is a universal facet of the human experience and deeply impacts our memories, emotions, and physiological processes. Despite its ubiquity, there are forms of grief not universally acknowledged or understood. The profound sadness stemming from the loss of a cherished pet often finds itself overshadowed, leaving many grappling in silence. This chapter addresses the specific details of pet-related grief, offering a comforting hand to those navigating its tumultuous waters.

The Hidden Heartache: Understanding Disenfranchised Grief

In a world that is constantly evolving, where norms shift and societies progress, certain emotions still find themselves pushed to the periphery. Disenfranchised grief, a term introduced by Dr. Kenneth Doka (an authority in grief counseling), describes sorrow that isn't readily acknowledged by society. It often arises when the loss in question doesn't align with societal expectations or norms.

Amidst this spectrum, the grief following a pet's loss stands prominent. Our attachment to pets is not just sentimental; it's underpinned by biology. Oxytocin, often called the "love hormone," surges in our system not just when we bond with fellow humans, but also with our pets. Such scientific findings challenge the societal hierarchy of grief that tends to overlook and underemphasize pet losses.

Alex's story resonates with many pet owners. "When Bruno, my golden retriever, passed away, I felt an immense void. He had been my loyal companion for years. Yet, when I tried sharing my pain at work, the reactions varied from bemusement to comments such as, 'It's just a dog. Why not get another?' Not only was I dealing with the loss, but also the additional pain of having my grief minimized."

The Invisible Struggle of Pet Grief Amid Societal Misunderstanding

Mourning a pet often feels akin to navigating through silent tempests. Society's lack of understanding or outright dismissiveness often leaves grieving pet owners wrestling with their emotions largely in isolation.

Every pet owner's journey is unique, but a common theme is the sting of societal disregard or misunderstanding. The nuances of this disenfranchised grief can be profoundly isolating. Comments such as "It was only an animal" or "Why don't you get a new one?" can magnify feelings of loneliness and devaluation.

Jake's experience sheds light on this: "When my tabby cat, Juju, passed away, the emptiness I felt was hard to put into words. He had been my steadfast companion during the loneliest chapters of my life. Yet, a well-meaning friend remarked, 'It's not like you lost a child.' Those words, though unintended, deepened my pain."

So, how can one navigate these turbulent waters of misunderstood grief?

1. **Embrace your emotions:** It begins with introspection. Recognize and honor your feelings. Understand that the bond you shared with your pet was genuine and the ensuing pain from the loss is just as real.

2. **Seek supportive communities:** In our digitally connected era, solace can be found in shared experiences. Numerous online forums and support groups dedicated to pet loss provide the opportunity for understanding and camaraderie.

3. **Consider therapy:** The therapeutic community is growing increasingly attuned to the depth of grief associated with pet loss. Speaking about your feelings

in a supportive environment can be an instrumental step toward healing.

Interactive Prompt: Recall a cherished memory with your pet. What emotions arise? How does this memory underline the depth and authenticity of your bond?

The Science Behind Sorrow: Validating the Intensity of Pet Grief

The role pets play in our lives isn't just sentimentally profound; it's also scientifically substantiated. Research highlights the depth of the human-animal bond. For instance, studies have shown that our brains react to pets in ways strikingly similar to how they respond to close human counterparts. This suggests that the emotional connections formed with our pets aren't just based on perceptions or sentiments, but are grounded in neurobiology. The release of oxytocin, often referred to as the "love hormone," isn't exclusive to human interactions. Engaging with our pets can trigger similar oxytocin surges, reinforcing the depth and authenticity of such bonds.

For various reasons, this biological reality often clashes with societal perceptions. Emily's experience reflects this dissonance: "When my parrot, Miko, passed away, a colleague casually remarked, 'But it's just a bird.' To me, Miko wasn't 'just a bird.' He was my companion during those late work nights, my confidant, and a source of solace during challenging times. The dismissal of my grief was heartbreaking."

Navigating this gap between personal experience and societal understanding is challenging, but awareness is the first step to bridging this divide. By shedding light on the neuroscientific foundations of the human-animal bond, we can pave the way toward broader societal recognition of the significance and intensity of pet grief.

Steps to Healing: From Self-compassion to Societal Acknowledgment

When faced with the dual challenges of personal grief and societal misunderstanding, healing requires both self-compassion and external validation. Here are some practical strategies to help navigate this multifaceted journey:

1. **Engage in memorial activities:** Activities like creating a scrapbook, holding a memorial service, or even planting a tree in memory of the pet can be therapeutic. These activities are tangible ways to honor the bond and facilitate the expression of grief.

Such rituals serve as a testament to the profound love shared and also act as anchors in the journey towards acceptance.

Interactive Prompt: Think of a cherished moment with your pet. How could you commemorate this memory in a tangible or symbolic manner?

2. **Educational outreach:** Sharing articles, research, or personal experiences can enlighten peers and acquaintances about the gravity of pet grief. This not only validates your own experiences, but can also pave the way for a more understanding and empathetic community.

3. **Mindfulness practices:** Techniques such as mindfulness-based stress reduction (MBSR) have been shown to alleviate grief-related stress. Coupled with self-care and intentional reflection, such practices can provide crucial support in managing the emotional complexities of pet loss.

In the midst of an often-inattentive society, it's imperative to remember that each bond shared with a pet is deeply personal. While intense, the grief serves as a reminder of the love that was shared. With time, understanding, and support, healing is not only possible, but a beautiful example of the resilience of the human spirit.

CHAPTER 7

Rebuilding Phase: Embracing Life and New Beginnings

"Though no one can go back and make a brand-new start, anyone can start from now and make a brand-new ending."

—— Carl Bard

The reality is that you will grieve forever. You will not "get over" the loss of a loved one; you will learn to live with it. You will heal and you will rebuild yourself around the loss you have suffered. You will be whole again, but you will never be the same. Nor should you be the same, nor would you want to.

— Elisabeth Kübler-Ross,
Psychiatrist and Author of *On Death and Dying*

As the setting sun casts its final golden hues, it prepares the canvas for a new dawn. Such is the nature of life, where endings make way for beginnings, even when faced with the devastating loss of a cherished pet. It's a continuous cycle, and grief is but a chapter in the grand tapestry of existence.

The emphasis in this chapter is on finding practical ways of moving forward. While the previous chapters were a deep dive into understanding and navigating the multifaceted emotions of grief, this chapter is about the actionable steps one can take to rebuild and renew. It's not about forgetting; it's about honoring the past, cherishing memories, and making space for new experiences.

From exploring the idea of adopting a new pet to reconnecting with hobbies and passions that might have taken a backseat during the grieving process, this chapter will provide a roadmap for those ready to take the first brave steps into the next phase of their journey.

We will delve into practical strategies, activities, and thought exercises designed to reignite a zest for life. These methods are grounded in both scientific research and real-life experiences, providing a balance between evidence-based approaches and genuine empathy.

Life, with its intricate blend of joys and sorrows, continues its march. This chapter is about joining that march once again, with an open heart, hope in your step, and a willingness to embrace new beginnings.

Embracing Renewal After Pet Loss

As the days turn into weeks and weeks into months, the acute pain of losing a cherished pet begins to fade into a dull ache. While the heartbreak remains, a moment comes when the thought of remaining in a state of perpetual mourning becomes more burdensome than the idea of moving forward. The desire to heal, find joy again, and seek new beginnings is the next step in rebuilding.

The journey of recovery and finding renewed purpose is unique to every individual. For some, it might involve adopting another pet; for others, it could mean dedicating time to causes close to their heart, like animal welfare or rescue operations. And then there are those who might find solace in something entirely different, like a newfound hobby or even a change in career.

There is a solid scientific foundation for the idea that engaging in activities, forming new connections, and setting goals can help individuals process grief and find meaning. According to a study in the Journal of Positive Psychology, engaging in new experiences, even small ones, can contribute to a more positive outlook and improved well-being during times of grief.

This chapter is not about hastening the grieving process or advocating for "moving on" quickly. Instead, it's about understanding that when the heart feels ready, there's a world of possibilities awaiting, full of potential moments of joy, laughter, and love.

Reflective Thought: What small new experiences can you introduce to your routine this week? Consider this an invitation to gradually invite renewal and joy back into your life.

One might ask, "How do I know I'm ready?" The answer is deeply personal. Some might hear an inner voice urging them to venture out of their cocoon of sorrow, while others might experience a more profound realization during a moment of reflection.

Sophia, a 40-year-old graphic designer, shared her story with us: "After months of grieving the loss of my cat, Luna, I was visiting a friend and saw a painting that took my breath away. I realized that while Luna had brought immense joy to my life, there were other avenues of happiness still open to me. This thought was both liberating and terrifying."

Finding the path forward doesn't mean forgetting the past. It's about cherishing the memories, honoring the bond, and opening oneself up to the potential of the future.

Acceptance and Integration: Honoring Their Legacy While Embracing the Future

The concept of acceptance is widely recognized in the world of grief counseling and psychology. It's often seen as the final stage in the grieving process. However, this doesn't mean it signals the end of grief. Rather, it is a shift in how we relate to and understand our loss.

Acceptance, in the context of losing a cherished pet, isn't about coming to terms with their absence in a way that feels dismissive or forgetful. It's about integrating the love and memories of that pet into a new understanding of life that can exist harmoniously with their memory.

The journey to acceptance is deeply personal and varies for each individual. For some, it's a slow process, punctuated with moments of reflection and remembrance. For others, it might be a more defined moment of clarity, where the sorrow gradually starts to take a backseat to feelings of gratitude and cherished memories.

"The pain passes, but the beauty remains."
— **Pierre-Auguste Renoir**

A study in the Journal of Personal and Social Psychology indicates that engaging in reflective practices and intentionally reminiscing about positive memories can facilitate emotional recovery during times of loss. This doesn't mean suppressing feelings of sadness, but rather balancing them with moments of gratitude and reflection.

Take the story of Elena, a school teacher who lost her bird, Percy: "One day, I found myself humming the tune Percy and I used to sing together. Instead of it making me sad, it brought a smile to my face. It was at that moment that I realized Percy's essence was still very much a part of my life."

The notion of integrating the memories of a lost pet involves creating a space where those memories can coexist with new experiences, opportunities, and joys. It's like building a bridge between the past and the present.

Some practical ways to facilitate acceptance and integration include:

1. **Memorial practices:** Create a dedicated space or ritual that honors your pet, whether it's a photo album, a corner with their favorite toys, or a yearly ritual on their birthday.
2. **Reflection and journaling:** Documenting feelings can provide an outlet and serve as a tribute to the journey of healing.
3. **Seek support:** Sharing stories and memories with others can help in realizing that the bond with the pet is everlasting and not confined to their physical presence.

At the heart of acceptance is the knowledge that love never truly ends. The physical presence of a pet might be gone, but the essence of what they brought into one's life remains. Embracing life after their passing doesn't mean leaving them behind, but carrying their memory forward into new days filled with potential, growth, and love.

Reflective Exercise: Take a moment to find a quiet space. With a pen and paper, jot down three cherished memories of your pet. Beside each memory, write a word or phrase that encapsulates the emotion attached to it. For example, if you recall the first time your cat curled up on your lap, the accompanying emotion might be "warmth" or "bonding." This exercise serves as a beautiful reminder of the profound connection you shared and the feelings that those memories still evoke.

This exercise provides readers with a proactive way to engage with their emotions, helping them process their grief and cherish the bond they had with their pet.

Navigating New Beginnings: Daily Routines, Rituals, and the Journey Ahead

One of the most daunting experiences after the loss of a cherished pet is facing the "every day." The routines that were once so full of moments of joy and bonding now feel different, altered by the void left behind. But as time progresses, these routines can transform into avenues of healing, memory, and even new beginnings.

1. Transitioning Back to Daily Routines

A sense of normalcy can provide a comforting structure during times of grief. It offers moments of respite and can act as an anchor. Here are a few steps to ease back into daily routines:

- **Gradual steps:** Start with small tasks. If you used to take morning walks, perhaps begin by simply stepping outside and breathing in the fresh air, even if just for a few minutes.
- **Seek support:** Talk to friends or family members. They can join you in some of these routines, offering company and understanding.
- **Alter routines:** If certain activities are too painful, consider slight modifications. If you used to play fetch in the park, maybe try a new form of exercise, like yoga or cycling, to mark a fresh start.

Prompt for Reflection: List three daily activities that you find comforting and three that you'd like to modify or change. This exercise can help you identify which routines to hold onto and which to adapt in light of your current feelings.

2. Establishing New Rituals

Creating new rituals can be therapeutic. They don't replace old ones, but offer a way to honor memories while introducing new experiences.

- **Memory box:** Collect mementos such as a collar, toys, or photos in a dedicated space. Visit this space whenever you wish to reminisce or connect.
- **Dedication:** Dedicate a heartfelt act in their memory that signifies their everlasting presence in your life, such as planting a bush or flower in your garden that blooms every year. Alternatively, penning a poignant poem or crafting a custom keepsake like a memorial locket can honor their spirit and keep them close to your heart.

3. Welcoming Another Pet

The thought of having another pet might evoke mixed emotions. Some may feel they're betraying their previous pet, while others might see it as a tribute. Here are some things to consider:

- **Personal readiness:** There's no universally right time. It's about when you feel ready to form a new bond, understanding it won't be a replacement but a distinct, new relationship.
- **Research:** Different breeds or species have different needs. Familiarize yourself with these to ensure a good fit for both you and the pet.
- **Adoption:** Consider adopting a pet. Many animals are in need of loving homes, and you could provide one, channeling your experience and love to a deserving new companion.

A New Chapter with Lila

Losing Belly and Sweepea was one of the most heartbreaking experiences our family had ever endured. Once lively with the playful antics of our beloved French bulldogs, our home suddenly felt unbearably quiet and empty. Rudy, who had been their companion, visibly wilted away in sorrow, losing his zest for life without his friends.

Then, something unexpected happened. A friend told us about Lila, a rescued French bulldog that urgently needed a home. Initially, we hesitated, still drowning in our grief. But there was something in Lila's eyes that quietly whispered to our mourning hearts.

From the moment Lila entered our home, things began to change. Her boundless energy and sweet, playful nature breathed a new life into Rudy, who, to our relief, began eating and playing again. He allowed Lila to groom him, and soon they were inseparable, sharing a beautiful bond that was healing to witness.

It wasn't only Rudy who benefited from Lila's presence. She brought back laughter to our home, helping our children and us find a path out of our darkness. With her around, joy seeped into our lives in unexpected moments, while the memories of Belly and Sweepea lingered lovingly in the background.

Lila taught us an invaluable lesson: Opening our hearts to new companionship didn't mean betraying our memories. Instead, it meant allowing our love to flow onwards.

Despite all of its challenges, life is also brimming with possibilities. While the pain of loss never truly vanishes, the capacity of the human heart to heal, adapt, and find joy again is profound. Embracing routines and rituals and considering new companionship can be gateways to rediscovering happiness, while always keeping your cherished memories alive.

CHAPTER 8

From Darkness to Light: Pet Loss Can't Be Solved, but It Can Be Survived

"In the tender journey of grief, it's not about finding a solution, but embracing the memories, honoring the love, and navigating through with grace."

— Evelyn Hartman

The journey through pet loss presents us with an emotional maze, one that isn't meant to be hastily maneuvered, but understood and traversed with patience.

Grief's intricate dance involves complex cognitive and emotional processes. Regions of the brain related to reward, motivation, and emotion regulation are activated, and our neural response to such losses demonstrates the fact that grief isn't merely an obstacle, but an inherent part of our human experience. It's an avenue through which we learn, adapt, and grow.

Navigating this path doesn't mean sidelining our pain. Rather, we must embrace the transformative potential it holds. This chapter looks more closely at the steps of this journey, offering insights into the shared human experience of loss and guiding us toward a renewed appreciation for life's ebb and flow.

Navigating the Emotional Labyrinth of Pet Loss

Pet loss is not a jigsaw puzzle waiting for the right pieces to fit in, or a math problem where a formula brings forth a solution. Instead, it is an emotional labyrinth. Every twist and turn, every dead-end and unexpected path represents a facet of the emotions felt during this journey.

Our brains' responses to grief activate areas associated with emotion regulation, memory, and reward. This is an intricate combination of reactions where the brain's plasticity comes into play, adapting to the emotional upheaval. This adaptation doesn't happen overnight; it is a gradual process shaped by personal experiences and coping mechanisms. The aftermath of pet loss doesn't follow a predetermined map, and that's perfectly okay.

Many people often seek a structured path to navigate this grief, looking for clear-cut answers. But, the journey of healing after the loss of a pet doesn't come with a one-size-fits-all blueprint. Instead, it involves introspection, support, understanding, and, most importantly, giving oneself the grace to heal in their own unique way.

Sarah, a dog lover and grief survivor, once shared, "When Frankly, my Labrador, passed away, I found solace not in forgetting or moving on swiftly, but in cherishing the moments we had and allowing myself to mourn in my own rhythm. The idea that healing required a timeline or a structured approach was a burden I learned to let go of."

As the neurons in our brains forge new connections, adapting to the absence of our cherished pets, we must recognize that the healing process is not about erasing the pain, but rather reshaping our relationship with it. It is about acknowledging our feelings, validating them, and realizing that there's no set path or time frame for healing.

Dr. Margaret M. Stroebe, a researcher specializing in bereavement, highlights the natural and necessary process of grieving. In her collaborative work, *Handbook of Bereavement: Theory, Research, and Intervention* (Stroebe, M.S., Stroebe, W. & Hansson, R.O. eds., 1993), she states, "grief is not a disorder, a disease, or a sign of weakness. It is an emotional, physical, and spiritual necessity, the price you pay for love. The only cure for grief is to grieve."

Embracing the multifaceted nature of this process can be liberating. Recognizing that the emotional labyrinth is not meant to entrap but to teach allows individuals to find their own waypoints, form their own coping strategies, and gradually, find light amidst the shadows.

To guide oneself through this journey, practical strategies can be employed:

1. **Journaling:** Documenting emotions, memories, and milestones in the healing journey can be therapeutic. This provides a canvas where raw emotions can be poured out, providing clarity and a space for reflection.

2. **Mindful meditation:** Bringing awareness to the present can be beneficial for grounding oneself, especially during overwhelming moments.

3. **Joining support groups:** Finding individuals who resonate with your journey can be comforting. It not only provides a platform for mutual understanding, but also provides perspective, as you have the opportunity to see the many ways people cope and adapt.

Understanding grief as a process and embracing its nonlinear nature can make the journey more manageable, leading individuals not to a destination, but a new beginning.

The Emotional Spectrum of Pet Loss

Losing a beloved pet is like navigating through a storm, and every emotion is as unpredictable as the chaotic waves. These emotions, ranging from grief to anger, are not neatly compartmentalized. Rather, they often overlap, intermingle, and sometimes even crash against one another.

1. **Grief:** This emotion is perhaps the most immediately recognized and understood. Grief is a natural response to loss, and it demonstrates the depth of the bonds we share with our pets. Some people may find themselves revisiting favorite memories or locations. They might catch themselves momentarily forgetting the pet is no longer there, and then feeling the weight of their absence all over again.

2. **Depression:** Beyond the initial grief lies a profound sadness. This emotion might manifest as listlessness, a lack of interest in activities, or even a sense of being adrift without an anchor. Sadness isn't merely about missing the pet; it's about adjusting to a world where they are no longer present.

3. **Guilt:** Many pet owners grapple with guilt, especially if they had to make difficult decisions regarding their pet's well-being or end-of-life care. Questions like "Did I do enough?" or "Could I have prevented this?" are common. Such feelings, while natural, can be debilitating if not addressed.

4. **Anger:** Anger might manifest in various ways—from frustration over the circumstances of the pet's passing

to resentment towards others who might not comprehend the depth of the loss. It's essential to understand that anger, in many cases, is a secondary emotion, serving as a protective layer over more vulnerable feelings, like hurt or sadness.

5. **Emptiness:** Perhaps one of the most challenging emotions to deal with is the sense of emptiness. The routines, the shared moments, and the unconditional love all contribute to a pet becoming an integral part of one's life. Their absence can create a vacuum that's hard to fill.

The complexity of these emotions can sometimes be overwhelming, but it's crucial to understand that they are valid, natural responses to loss. Accepting and acknowledging them is the first step towards navigating the tumultuous experience of pet loss.

From a scientific perspective, emotions are crucial for the brain to process significant events. An article from Forbes, referencing the insights of Dr. Joan Halifax, suggests that emotions have developed over time as our adaptive responses to various environmental challenges (Wiest, B., 2018. *This Is The Psychological Reason Why Some People Are So Hard On Themselves.* Forbes). In the context of pet loss, these emotions serve as the brain's mechanisms for processing the sudden absence, adapting to a changed reality, and paving a way forward.

One approach to managing these emotions is the practice of "emotional labeling." Dr. Matthew Lieberman, a psychologist at UCLA, found that simply naming our emotions can have a calming effect on the brain. When feeling overwhelmed, taking a moment to internally acknowledge "I am feeling sad" or "I am feeling angry" can serve as a grounding exercise.

Another strategy is seeking professional counseling or joining pet bereavement groups. Sharing feelings and experiences with others can create a supportive space where emotions are neither judged nor dismissed, but instead genuinely understood.

Above all, it's imperative to remember that there's no right or wrong way to feel. Every individual's journey is unique. By acknowledging and accepting the range of emotions, you can take the first step in the healing process.

Embracing Grief Instead of Evading It

In the modern age, there's a prevalent inclination to view challenges and pain as problems to be solved swiftly. There's a pill for headaches, a manual for fixing appliances, and an app for almost every inconvenience in life. However, when confronted with the pain of losing a pet, many are taken aback by the absence of a straightforward "solution."

This is an understandable response. The instinctual urge to alleviate pain is potent and deeply rooted in the human psyche. But grief doesn't lend itself to simple fixes. It demands acknowledgment, patience, and, most crucially, a change in perspective.

The very idea of "solving" grief presupposes that it's an unwanted intruder in one's life. But grief is actually an expression of our love. It's the heart's way of recognizing the depth of the bond that was shared with the pet. Instead of viewing it as an adversary, one might consider it a companion on the journey of healing.

Embracing grief doesn't mean wallowing in sadness or being consumed by it. It means allowing oneself to feel, to reminisce, to cry, and even to smile at fond memories. It's a process of honoring the bond shared with the pet and acknowledging its significance in one's life.

From a scientific standpoint, psychologists like Dr. Susan David, who has extensively researched emotional agility, highlight the importance of facing one's emotions head-on. In her work, she explains that trying to suppress or deny feelings can lead to more prolonged emotional pain. By contrast, acknowledging and embracing one's feelings can foster resilience and a more profound emotional healing.

A practical strategy to help you adopt this perspective is journaling. Penning down thoughts and feelings about the pet, memories shared, and the various emotions experienced can be therapeutic. It allows for introspection and provides a safe space for raw, unfiltered expressions of grief. Over time, revisiting these entries can offer insights into the evolution of one's emotional landscape and the progress made in the healing journey.

Additionally, seeking support from therapists specializing in grief counseling or participating in support groups can facilitate this shift in perspective. Hearing others' stories and sharing one's own can cultivate a sense of solidarity, reinforcing the idea that grief is a universal experience, even though it is uniquely personal in its manifestations.

In the end, the journey through grief isn't about arriving at a destination where the pain is entirely gone. It's about learning to coexist with the memories, cherishing the bond that was, and gradually finding joy in new beginnings. By reframing grief as a passage rather than a problem, one can navigate the waves of emotion with grace and resilience, discovering light amidst the shadows.

Conclusion

"Healing is not about moving on from grief, but rather learning to live with it."

—— James Baldwin

Throughout this guide, we've delved deep into the experience of pet loss, uncovering layers of emotions, from profound grief to glimmers of hope. The loss of a beloved pet is a deeply personal journey, unique to every individual. We've discussed the fact that grief is multifaceted, encompassing a range of feelings such as sadness, guilt, anger, and emptiness.

We've emphasized that pet loss isn't a straightforward issue that demands a solution. Instead, it's a complex emotional process that requires patience, understanding, and time. Embracing this journey rather than looking for quick fixes is central to genuine healing.

As you embark on this journey, you're not alone. Many have walked this path before and have found solace, healing, and even joy in their lives once again. While it might seem impossible now, there are numerous testimonies from individuals who have learned to cherish the memories of their pets and find new purpose and happiness.

Science supports the notion that humans possess an incredible capacity for resilience. Neuroplasticity, the brain's ability to adapt and change, provides hope that, over time, the sharp edges of grief can soften. With effort and support, it's possible to rewire our responses and find new avenues for happiness.

The journey of healing isn't about forgetting or replacing the lost companion. Instead, it's about honoring their memory, cherishing the moments shared, and making space for new experiences without letting go of the old. Remember, the depth of your grief is a testament to the depth of your love.

In closing, find solace in the knowledge that while the pain of loss might linger, it doesn't define the entirety of your existence. With each passing day, as you actively engage in the healing process, you're taking steps towards a future filled with renewed purpose, joy, and love.

May you find strength in your memories, courage in your journey, and peace in the understanding that love, once given and received, remains eternal. Your beloved pet's legacy lives on in every heartbeat, every tear shed, and every smile that recalls the beautiful moments shared. Embrace this legacy, for it's the most beautiful tribute to a bond that time can never erase.